This Coloring Book Belongs to:

color test page

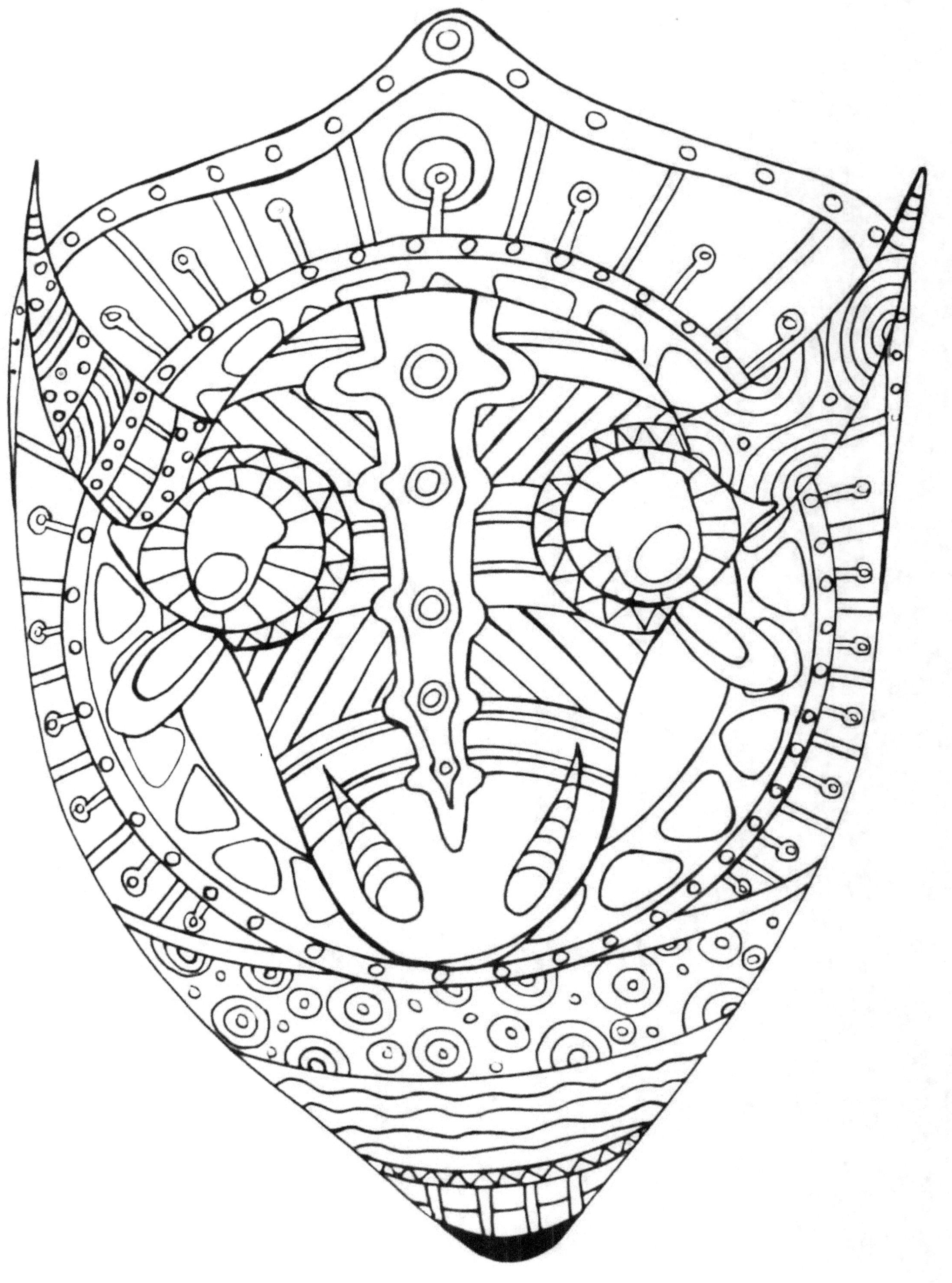

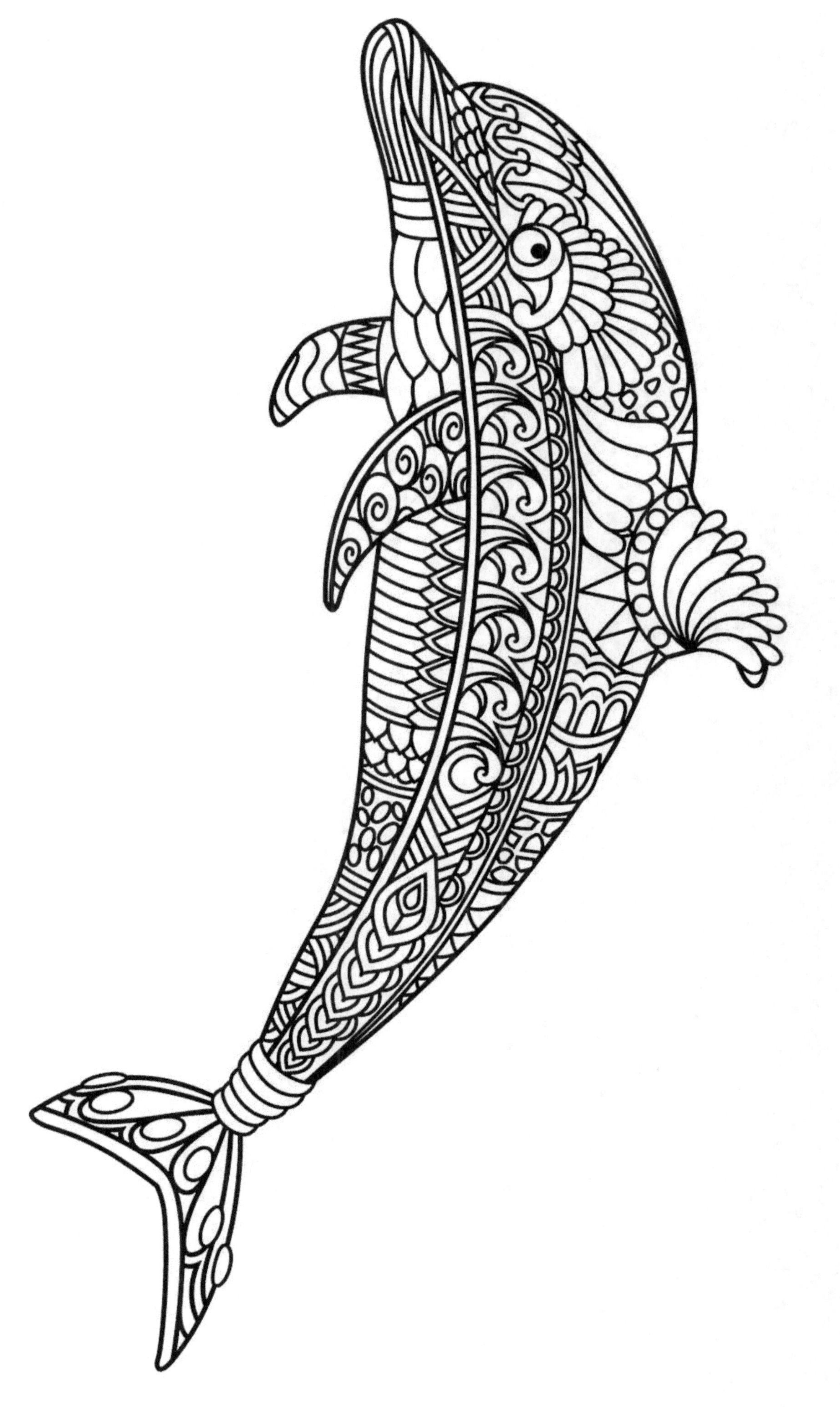

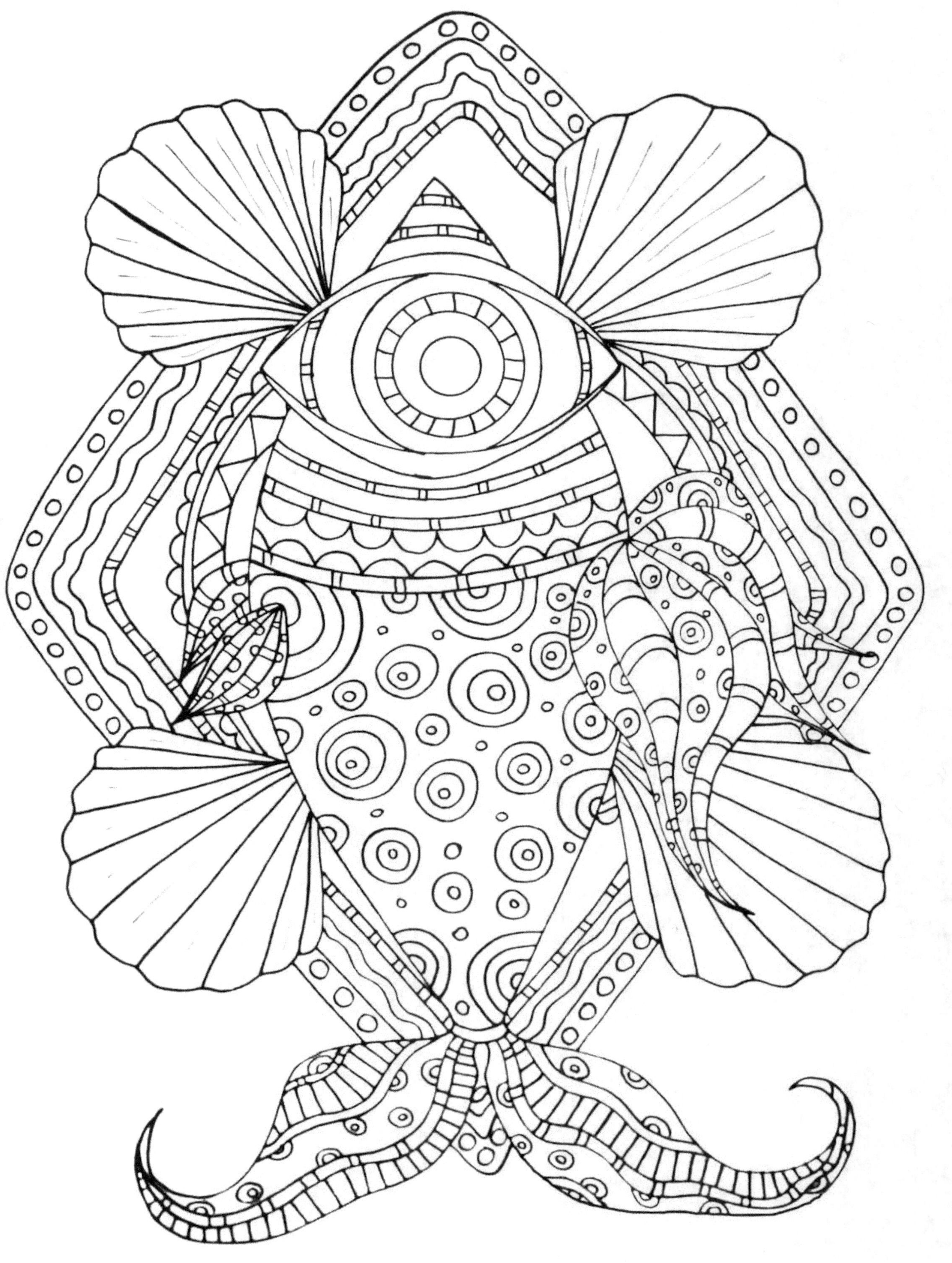

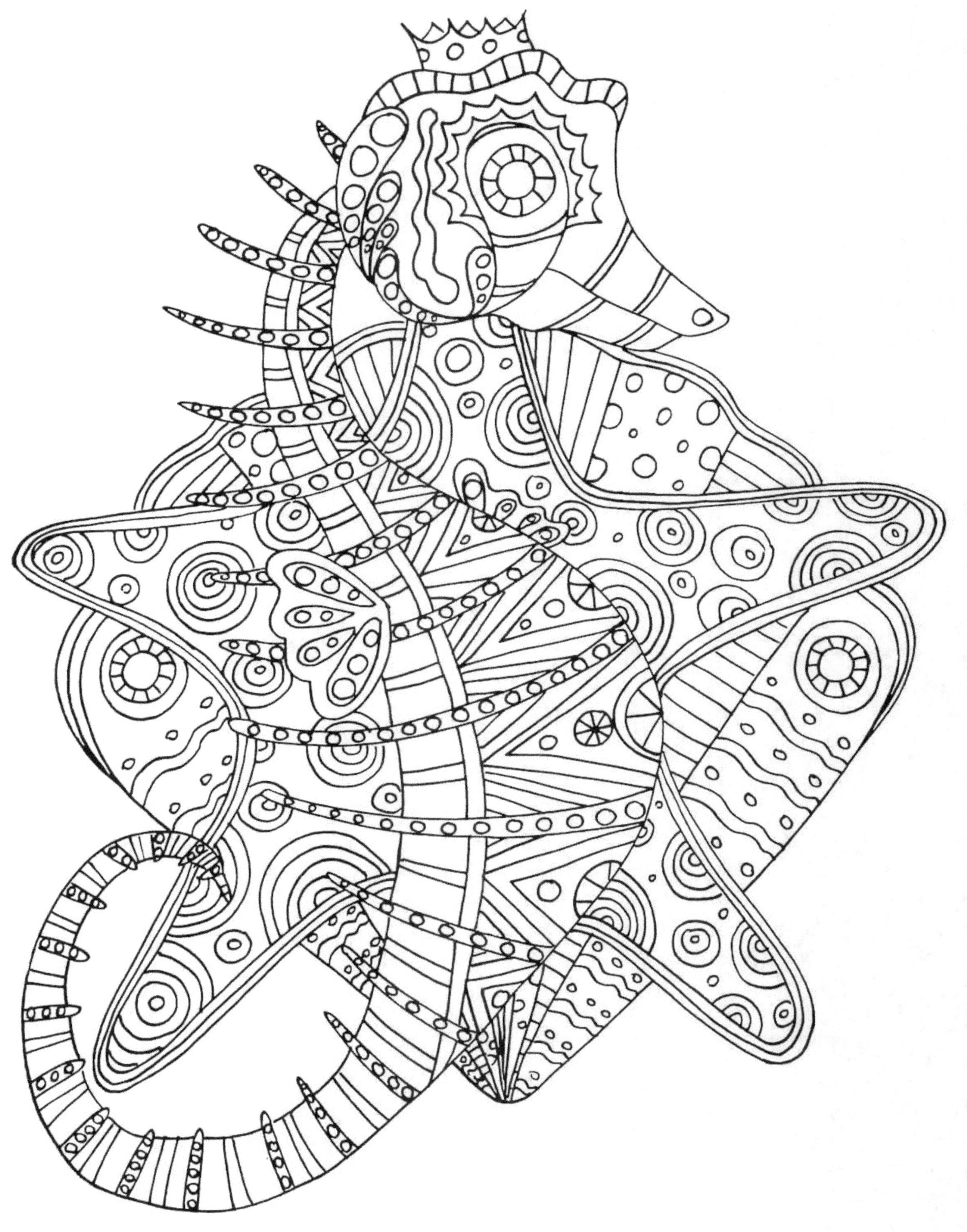

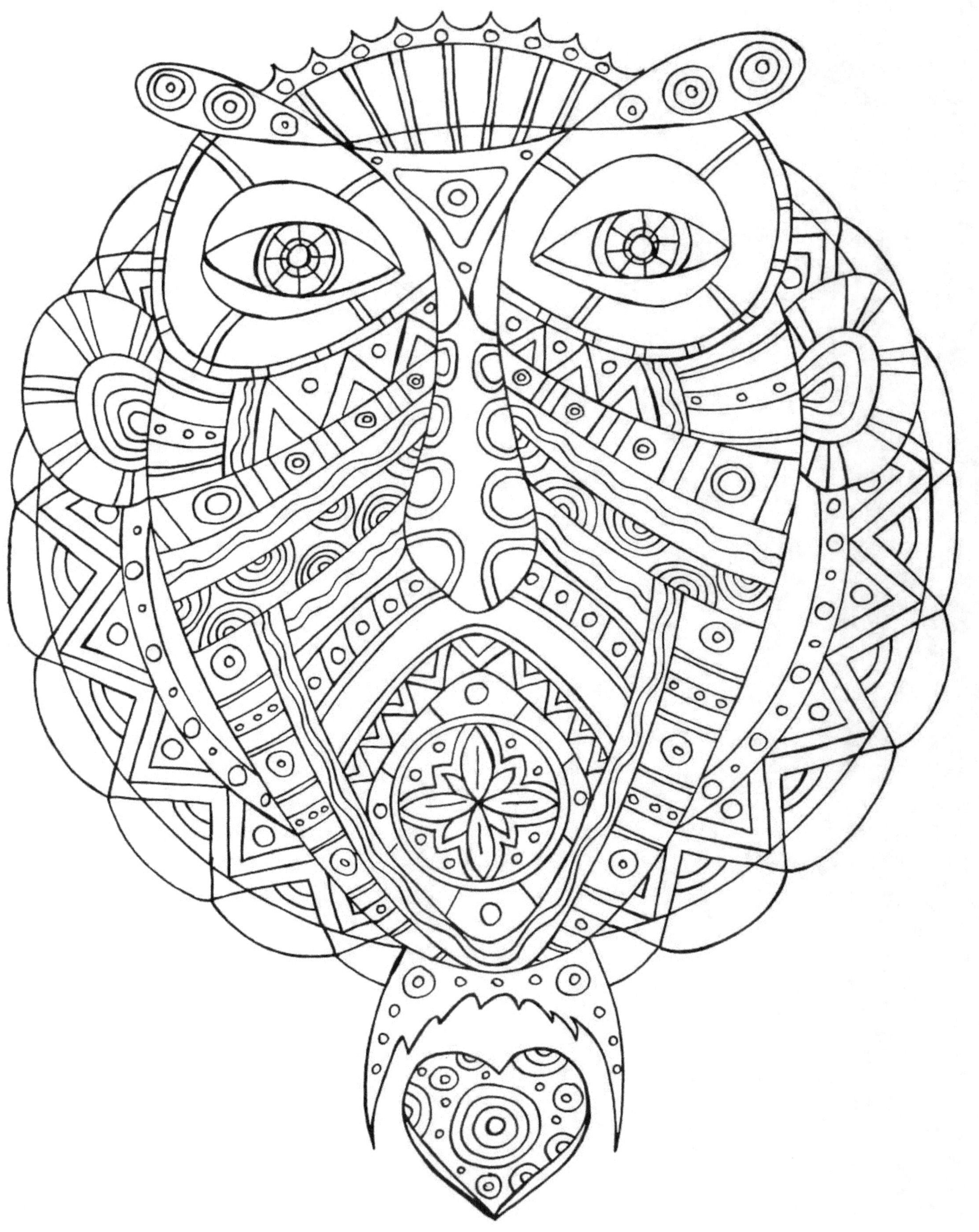

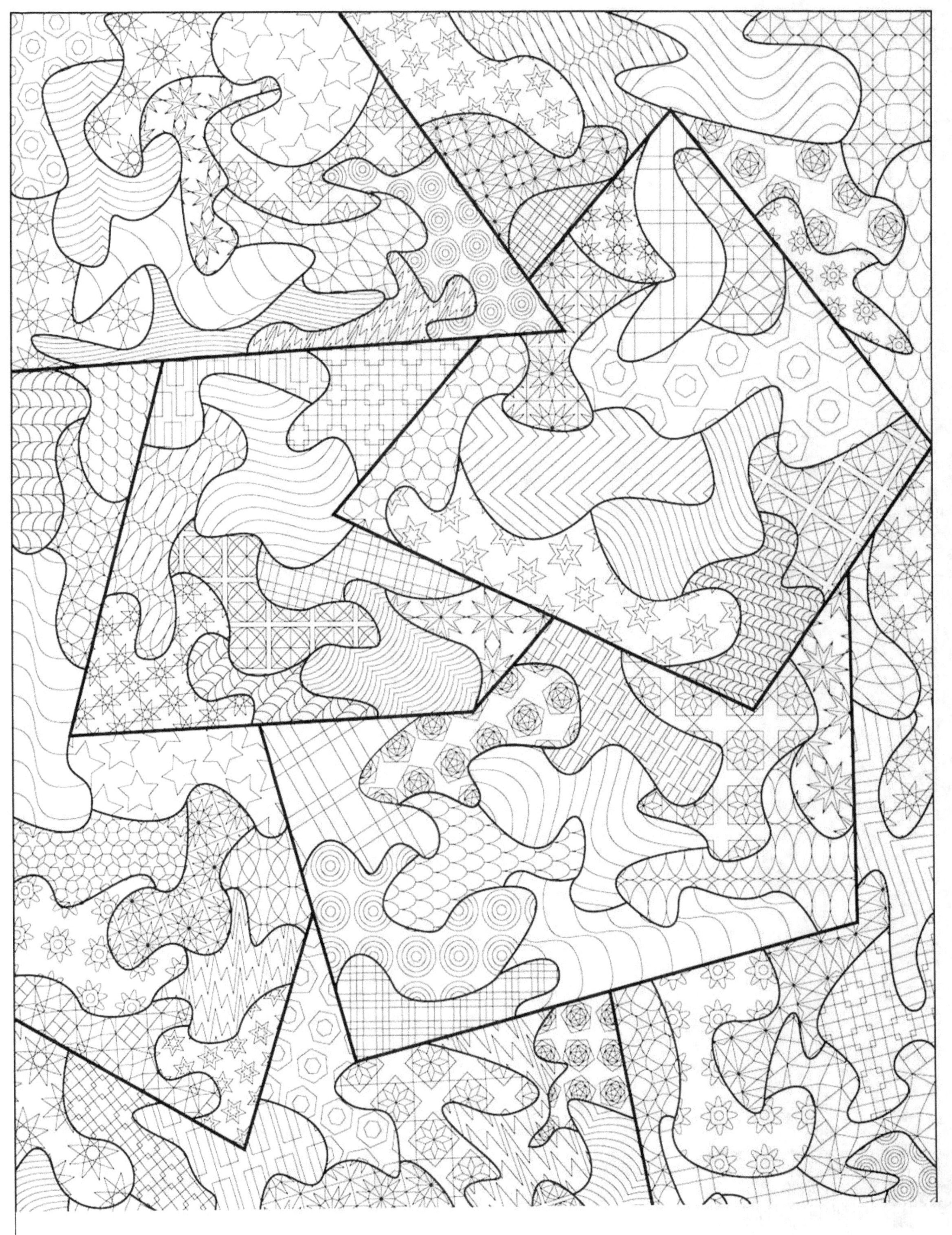